IN THEIR OWN WORDS

THE GREAT DEPRESSION

A Primary Source History

Stanley Schultz

GARETH**STEVENS**

GS

PUBLISHING

A Member of the WRC Media Family of Companies

Cover photos:
Top: *Herbert Hoover, president of the United States in the early years of the Great Depression, was given much of the blame by the American people for the nation's economic woes.*
Bottom: *A migrant family walks on the highway from Idabel to Krebs, Oklahoma, in search of work.*

CONTENTS

Above: *A photograph of a Farm Security Administration borrower taken during the 1930s.*

Right: *A poor farming couple, Faro and Doris Caudill, from the state of Oklahoma. Oklahoma was one of the hardest hit states during the Great Depression.*

O ctober 29, 1929, was known ever after as "Black Tuesday." The nation was stunned by the greatest economic disaster in U.S. history. Panicked Wall Street investors rushed to sell their stocks at any price, but they found no buyers. The stock market crash echoed across the country. Americans lost millions of dollars over the next few weeks. One of the world's richest nations was fast going broke. In 1929, the national income stood at $87 billion; by 1933, it had plummeted to $40 billion. An economic crisis that became known as the Great Depression was in full swing.

The drastic decline in the economy spread across the world, bringing widespread poverty. International trade almost ceased. Agricultural countries were impoverished, and in industrialized countries production fell, causing massive job losses. Almost one in four U.S. workers was unemployed. People lost their homes because they could not pay for them. They scavenged for food or lined up to accept charity donations. Others took to the road looking for work and ended up in shanty towns outside big cities. The bewildered people wanted someone or something to blame. Many aimed their anger toward bankers, stockbrokers, and businesspeople. Others blamed President Herbert Hoover, who seemed unwilling or unable to halt the economic plunge. They believed that Hoover and the people who ran the financial industry had brought on the stock market crash. And they believed the crash had created the Great Depression. They were wrong. The crash actually just exposed long-standing problems that most Americans had ignored. During the 1920s, a wide chasm had opened between a few wealthy Americans and the majority who lived on fairly low incomes. Small producers and sellers had been increasingly unable to compete with large companies. Yearly, thousands of farm families teetered on the edge of bankruptcy. Unregulated banks took economic risks that threatened their customers' savings accounts.

Above: *As many farms went broke during the Great Depression, tools were sold for a pittance.*

Hoover's federal government responded to the Great Depression with talk, not action. Officials tried to calm rising panic by telling the public that prosperity was just around the corner. Humorist Will Rogers observed: "If we could have eaten and digested optimistic prediction during 1930, we would have been the fattest nation on Earth."

Hoover believed government should not regulate businesses but should encourage them instead to become more efficient. He opposed government spending on projects that might compete with private business enterprises. He also rejected the notion that the federal government should set up relief programs or directly assist farmers who were trying to hold onto their land.

Above: *One of the lasting legacies of the Great Depression was a shift away from small, family-owned farms toward large-scale agricultural businesses.*

Above: *Towns and cities across the United States saw outbreaks of violence between the unemployed and the employed as people sometimes literally fought for jobs.*

Below: *Sharecroppers at work in the fields in Virginia.*

He urged charities and local governments to help the poor and unemployed. But voluntary relief efforts could not hold back the tide of economic losses. Charities and local governments were as broke as the Wall Street investors. Something new and different had to happen.

That "something new" followed the 1932 presidential campaign. Democrat and reform-minded New York Governor Franklin Delano Roosevelt, popularly known as FDR, ran against Republican Hoover. FDR won by a large margin and immediately promised a "New Deal" for the American people. During the rest of the decade, the New Deal set up a large number of federal government programs. Roosevelt's "New Dealers" spent billions of dollars on unemployment relief programs, payments to small farmers, and massive public works projects. They also introduced major reforms to benefit factory workers, the poor, the elderly, and the environment.

FDR became a great hero to many people but a villain to others. His opponents said he had built a socialist welfare state and shattered the tradition of individual competition. A minority of citizens demanded even more extreme changes. But quick-fix proposals by communists and others alarmed a public that was more fearful of domestic revolution than at any other time since the Civil War of the 1860s. Most people regarded FDR as their personal champion and the savior of capitalism (an economic system in which production and distribution of goods come from private ownership of resources) in the Untied States. One fact was certain: The New Deal did not solve the Great Depression's economic problems. By the late 1930s, the economy faltered again. Unemployment began to rise.

Events in Europe and Asia shifted attention to the U.S. role in world affairs. Most Americans wanted to remain neutral when war erupted in Europe in late 1939. Those hopes collapsed when Japan attacked the U.S. Navy at Pearl Harbor, Hawaii, on December 7, 1941. The United States' entry into World War II jump-started the U.S. economy. Wartime production put Americans back to work. World War II accomplished what all the New Deal relief and reform programs could not.

The United States was a vastly different society following the Great Depression than it had been before the crash. Most Americans started to look to Washington, D.C., for solutions to their problems. The president became the prime architect of domestic and foreign policies. Although Americans would continue to debate the virtues of "big government" versus individual and local responsibility, the legacies of the Great Depression and the New Deal shadowed the U.S. domestic and foreign policies from World War II into the early years of the twenty-first century.

Above: John Steinbeck's novel, The Grapes of Wrath, is about a poor family who left the Oklahoma Dust Bowl in a vain search for a better life in California.

Left: An unemployed farm worker takes to the road in search of work.

Above: As the U.S. government became involved in World War II—first through aid, then directly—more women were brought into the workforce.

Many Americans believed that the stock market crash of 1929 caused the Great Depression. But the crash actually revealed underlying problems that led to the Great Depression. The rich enjoyed vastly larger incomes than the majority of citizens. Overspending pushed many consumers into debt. A handful of big businesses dwarfed their smaller competitors, while the banking system was unstable. The nation's farmers were failing at a quickening pace. And other countries owed far more to the United States than they could pay.

Below: *Diagram showing the "bull" (upward spike) and "bear" (downward spike) patterns found in stock market trading. During a depression, traders say we have entered a "bear" market.*

DOLLARS COME CRASHING DOWN

At the start of 1929, *The New York Times* reviewed the economics of the United States for the previous year and noted that it had been twelve months "of unprecedented advance" and "wonderful prosperity." That autumn, the country's leading economist said the nation was marching along "a permanently high plateau of economic progress." One week later, October 24, 1929, the United States saw the start of its greatest economic crisis. This crisis was called "Black Thursday." The price of stocks on New York City's Wall Street Stock Exchange fell so rapidly that investors rushed to sell their stocks, even if it meant accepting a loss. Yet the following day, President Hoover assured the people. He said, "The fundamental business of the country . . . is on a sound and properous basis." His words did not stop the panic that investors were feeling. Five days later, on October 29 (a day known as Black Tuesday), there was another rush to sell stocks. Within two weeks, Americans had lost about thirty billion dollars.

WHAT CAUSED THE CRASH?

Stock prices rose steadily for the five years leading up to the crash. More people were buying than selling stocks. Economists call this a "bull" market. A "bear" market occurs when more people are selling, and it causes stock prices to fall. Many Americans saw the booming bull market as a sign of a healthy economy. Many people believed they could buy stocks and get rich

"Stock prices virtually exploded yesterday, swept downward with gigantic losses in the most disastrous trading day in the stock market's history. . . . Bid prices placed by bankers, industrial leaders, and brokers . . . were crashed through violently . . . in a day of . . . confusion. Groups of men, with here and there a woman, stood about inverted glass bowls all over the city yesterday watching spools of ticker tape unwind, and as the tenuous paper with its cryptic numbers grew longer at their feet, their fortunes shrunk. Others sat . . . in the customers' rooms of brokerage houses and watched a motion picture of waning wealth as the day's quotations moved silently across a screen. . . . There were no smiles. There were no tears either. Just the camaraderie of fellow sufferers. Everybody wanted to tell his neighbor how much he had lost. Nobody wanted to listen. It was too repetitious a tale."

On October 30, 1929, *The New York Times* described the Wall Street disaster of the previous day.

quickly. Because they didn't necessarily have money to buy stocks, they bought "on margin." That means, they borrowed the money from banks with a down payment of about 10 percent. They believed the price of the stocks would rise, and then they could sell the stocks, repay the banks, and still have money left over. When stock prices collapsed, however, investors could not pay back what they owed. The result was financial ruin.

THE UNITED STATES IN 1929

Many Americans may have wanted to get rich quick but few did. The

New York Daily
Investment News
12,894,650 Day Smashes Old Peak by 4 Million
STOCK MARKET CRISIS OVER
Stock Houses Survive Worst Day in History

WORST STOCK CRASH STEMMED BY BANKS;
12,894,650-SHARE DAY SWAMPS MARKET;
LEADERS CONFER, FIND CONDITIONS SOUND

Above: *Many papers prematurely heralded the end of the crash.*

Left: *The 1920s were a period of great prosperity and luxury for many Americans.*

TIME LINE
1929

AUGUST 21
Wall Street Journal predicts that for the stock market "the outlook for the fall months seems brighter than at any time in recent years."

SEPTEMBER 1
Price of a seat (allowing a person to buy and sell stocks) on the New York Stock Exchange hits all-time high of $625,000.

SEPTEMBER 30
The month sets an all-time record of $670 million in stockbrokers' loans to people to buy stocks "on margin."

"All over America . . . scrub-women, porters, elevator boys, typists . . . the whole population, rich and poor . . . fell a prey to the consuming craze for [stock] speculation. It seemed as if . . . success and prosperity could be had without knowledge or industry. . . . People were living in a world of illusion. . . .

After the crash, several writers . . . sought to explain the heavy fall. . . . Prices fell (writers declared) simply because a mob of stupid and ignorant speculators . . . suddenly took fright and began to sell. This explanation will not hold water. As a matter of fact, the mob of small speculators held on till the last moment, hoping desperately that . . . [stocks] would soon recover."

English economist Francis W. Hirst tried to make sense of the crash and to explain the American public's mood during the years before October, 1929.

Above: *The "Roaring Twenties" was a term used to describe the post World War I decade, which saw the introduction of cars including the Ford Model T.*

majority of citizens earned less money than they needed to live comfortably. Businesses started letting people with lower incomes buy houses, automobiles, and electrical appliances on credit. That meant they could buy things and pay for them a little at a time. When the crash occured, people could not pay their bills, and this drove the economy into chaos. If the people weren't paying the businesses, the businesses couldn't pay their bills either.

Income differences also damaged the nation's economic health and increased the length of the Great Depression. Throughout the 1920s, the difference between the yearly incomes of the rich and poor grew larger. An unequal distribution of the size and power of American

businesses also hurt the economy. By 1929, about six hundred corporations controlled nearly two-thirds of the national wealth. Company mergers in the railroad, steel, automobile, food packing, clothing, financial investment, and utility businesses had driven many small business owners close to the edge of failure. After the crash, the big corporations managed to limp through the Great Depression. Small businesspeople could not. Said one writer, "There are men and woman who have no control over discount rates, or credit, or manipulation of bull markets and bear markets, yet they are the first victims of the battles fought in those high and mysterious regions."

BANKING ON SUCCESS—AND LOSING
The 1929 crash unveiled another long-standing problem in the U.S. economy. The nation's banking system was in trouble. Few federal

"The figures [for 1929] reveal . . . nearly 6 million families, or more than 21 percent of the total, had incomes less than $1,000. About 12 million families, or more than 42 percent, had incomes less than $1,500. . . . Thus it appears that 0.1 percent of the families at the top received practically as much [income] as 42 percent of the families at the bottom of the scale. . . . At 1929 prices, a family income of $2,000 may perhaps be regarded as sufficient to supply only basic necessities. . . . More than 16 million families were below this standard of expenditures."

Economists at the Brookings Institution reported about income differences in *America's Capacity to Consume* (1934).

Above: *Angry investors surround a bank in 1929. It had just gone bust, and few of its investors would receive any compensation at all.*

TIME LINE
1929

OCTOBER 4
Arthur Cutten, head of the largest stock speculation companies, sees no end in sight for "bull markets" that could support brokers' loans up to $12 billion.

OCTOBER 29
More than 16.4 million shares of stock exchanged at rapidly falling prices, setting a record that lasted for the next four decades.

or state regulations existed to oversee bankers' actions. During the 1920s, businesspeople eager for profits opened thousands of new banks. Many lacked adequate money reserves. Between 1923 and 1929, banks across the country failed at the rate of two per day, but the general rising prosperity masked those failures. The onset of the crash made a bad situation even worse, and banks failed at an even more rapid rate.

THEY CAN'T PAY US

World War I (1914–1918) turned the United States into a creditor nation. Other countries owed the United States money. An international "gold standard" meant that each dollar in circulation had to be supported by gold of the same value. The United States expected other countries to pay debts either

in gold bullion or by buying more American-made products. This worked when other nations had enough gold, could sell their products to the United States, and could buy U.S. goods at fairly low prices. But the United States enacted two high tariffs (taxes on foreign-made products)—one in

Above: *The dollar had become one of the strongest currencies in the world before the crash.*

"Probably the banks would have collapsed anyhow, so widely had their funds been invested in questionable bonds and mortgages, so widely had they been mismanaged . . . so lax were the standards imposed upon them in many states, and so great was the strain upon the national economy of sustaining the weight of obligations which rested in their hands. At any rate, here at the heart of the national debt-and-credit structure, a great rift appeared and quickly widened. . . . All over the country, there began a whispering, barely audible at first, then louder and louder: 'Trouble's coming. . . . Better get your money out of the bank.' The murmur ran among the bankers: 'Trouble's coming. Better sell your bonds and get cash before it's too late.' The financial machinery of the country began to freeze into rigidity, the industrial and commercial machinery to slow down."

Widely read journalist Frederick Lewis Allen reported on the nation's banking problems in *Since Yesterday: The Nineteen-Thirties in America* (1940).

Left *Jack Whinery and his large family, Pie Town, New Mexico.*

Above: *Farmers borrowed heavily to buy machinery, but they had no way of paying back the money.*

"The worldwide depression has affected the countries of Europe more severely than our own. . . . From . . . the fall in the price of foreign commodities and the lack of confidence in economic and political stability abroad, there is an abnormal movement of gold into the United States, which is lowering the credit stability of many foreign countries. These and other difficulties abroad diminish buying power for our exports and in a measure are the cause of our continued unemployment and continued lower prices to our farmers."

President Herbert Hoover's speech on June 20, 1931, emphasized a cause of the Great Depression that went beyond the impact of the stock market crash.

1922 and another in 1930. U.S. industrialists raised the prices of goods they sold overseas. By 1930, Europe was also hit by depression. European gold supplies dwindled fast, and there was no way to pay what the United States was owed. This prolonged the Great Depression in the United States.

FARMING FOR FAILURE

Until the 1920s, more Americans lived on farms and in small towns than in cities. Agriculture appeared to be in good shape, and production was rising. But many farmers found themselves squeezed between high operating costs and low prices for produce, and imported products presented stiff competition. Many farmers borrowed money to rent or buy farm machinery. The average farm incomes fell. These economic losses drove workers from the nation's farms. Of those who remained, fewer owned the land they farmed. Instead, they were tenants, renting the land they worked and barely making a living. Bad farming methods, such as a lack of crop rotation, poor irrigation, and overfarming, meant farming was headed for disaster. The crash revealed the situation, and the farmers' plight was a major cause of the Great Depression. By 1933, lenders were repossessing twenty thousand farms each month.

Above: *Small farms like this one in Bridgetown, New Jersey, were the hardest hit during the Depression. As prices for their goods dropped, farmers ran up huge debts, and many eventually deserted their farms.*

TIME LINE
1929—1930

1929
President Hoover creates Federal Farm Board to promote sales of goods through cooperatives (voluntary organizations of farmers who pooled their resources) but fails to provide sufficient funding for program.

1931
Hoover imposes one-year moratorium (delay) on European reparations and war debts.

1930
Hoover calls White House conference and secures promises from leading manufacturers to maintain employment, wages, and prices; employers try, but within months they have to reduce wages and fire workers.

Years of drought in farming regions added to the problem. Storms during the 1930s ripped off drought-loosened topsoil, making the land barren.

Government subsidies were set up to help farmers, but in practice they benefited big corporations rather than poor farmers.

Left: *A family of sharecroppers chop cotton on rented land near White Plains, Greene County, Georgia.*

"The economic prospects of agriculture have been changed by . . . the great decrease in exports of farm products and by progress in technique. There has been no increase in crop acreage for fifteen years, nor in acre-yields of the crops as a whole for 30 years, yet agricultural production has increased about 50 percent. . . . The advancing efficiency . . . is due principally to the increased use of power machinery . . . and to the application of scientific knowledge. . . . The result of these changing forces has been a volume of agricultural production in excess of market demands, and this . . . affords a partial explanation of the net loss in farm population."

This portion of the *President's Research Committee on Social Trends* highlighted the existing problems of farmers prior to the devastating impact of the crash on the farm economy.

Above: *A bread line beside the Brooklyn Bridge approach in New York, 1931.*

From 1929 to 1933, a deepening Great Depression drove millions of Americans into despair. In cities and towns, the numbers of unemployed and homeless people rapidly grew. Drought and dust storms forced farmers from their land, putting them on the road in search of a better life elsewhere. The federal government seemingly refused to act to solve the crisis. In the presidential campaign of 1932, a desperate nation sought new political leadership.

> "We tried to struggle along living day by day. Then I couldn't pay the rent. I had a little car. . . . I sold it for $15 in order to buy some food for the family. . . . Finally people started to talk me into going into the relief. They had open soup kitchens . . . you had to . . . stand there . . . to get a bowl of soup. . . . I was so downcasted that I couldn't think of anything. . . . I went around trying to find a job as a salesman. They wouldn't hire me on account of my age. I was just like dried up."
>
> **Interview of Ben Isaacs, a successful clothing salesman until he lost all his money in the stock market crash.**

BREAD LINES AND SOUP KITCHENS

By 1932, more than thirteen million people were out of work, or nearly 25 percent of the labor force. A number of people often went for months without finding even part-time employment. People were starving because there were so many unemployed, and local governments were unable to help everyone. Private charities tried to feed the needy by setting up soup kitchens. Accustomed to taking care of themselves, men and women who stood in these "bread lines" waiting for food felt embarrassed and ashamed at having to accept such help.

NO PLACE LIKE HOME

By 1933, unable to pay their monthly mortgages, home owners

were losing their houses at the rate of one thousand each day. Renters found it equally difficult to keep a home because losing a job meant they couldn't pay rent. Some people managed to retain their homes by taking in lodgers, or people who would rent a room. Those who did have a place to stay often lived in constant fear of losing it.

A large number of Americans searched for work in other parts of the country by illegally riding on trains. A temporary job might earn them a few dollars, then they "hopped a freight car" on the next train. Between two and three million men, women, and teenagers moved about the nation during the 1930s. Some who wandered from place to place did not have families. Others left home to reduce the financial burden on their families. And still others left because they felt like the failure was their own, and they could not face their loved ones any longer. At the edges of large cities,

Left: *Sugarcane workers resting at the noon hour, Rio Piedras, Puerto Rico.*

> "I'm a boy of 12 years. I want to tell you about my family. My father hasn't worked for 5 months. He went plenty times to relief, he filled out application. They won't give us anything. I don't know why. Please you do something. We haven't paid 4 months rent. Everyday the landlord rings the door bell, we don't open the door for him. We are afraid that we will be put out, been put out before, and don't want to happen again. We haven't paid the gas bill, and the electric bill, haven't paid grocery bill for 3 months. My father he staying home. All the time he's crying because he can't find work. I told him why are you crying daddy, and daddy said why shouldn't I cry when there is nothing in the house. I feel sorry for him. . . . Please answer right away because we need it or we will starve. Thank you. God bless you."

An anonymous Chicago boy wrote this letter in 1936 to "Mr. and Mrs. Roosevelt in Washington, D.C."

TIME LINE
1930–1931

1930
Congress enacts the Hawley-Smoot Tariff, the highest in history, that quickly reduces world trade and results in higher rates of unemployment for U.S. workers.

1931
"Food riots" occur in Minneapolis and other cities. March: Three thousand unemployed workers riot at the Ford Motor Company in River Rouge, Michigan.

1931
New York sets up a Temporary Emergency Relief Administration (first state agency of its kind) to provide unemployment relief in the face of federal inaction; by April 1932, more than 750,000 New York City dwellers are dependent on city relief.

1931
Late in the year, Hoover appoints the Organization on Unemployment Relief whose chairman admits he does not know how many people are unemployed and counsels against federal relief.

makeshift housing made from shipping crates, cardboard boxes, and aluminum sheets sprang up to house the unemployed and the many travelers. These shantytowns were often called "Hoovervilles," after President Hoover, whom they believed had failed them.

DUST BOWL

The forces of nature, along with the loss of jobs, put Americans on the move during the Great Depression. For more than eight years (1931–1939), the worst drought ever to hit the United States plagued midwestern and southern Great Plains states. These areas became known as the Dust Bowl. Crops died, the parched and loosened topsoil blew away, and huge dust storms swept across the nation from Texas and Oklahoma all the way to North Dakota. A yellow-brownish haze or dark cloud of dirt several stories high could sometimes be seen. By 1934, the dust storms affected twenty-seven states and covered more than 75

Left: *Boys sitting on a truck parked at a labor camp in Robston, Texas.*

April 25 and August 6, 1934, Wednesday
"Last weekend was the worst dust storm we ever had. . . . Many days this spring, the air is just full of dirt coming, literally, for hundreds of miles. . . . The drought and dust storms are something fierce. As far as one can see are brown pastures and fields, which, in the wind, just rise up and fill the air with dirt. It tortures animals and humans, makes housekeeping an everlasting drudgery, and ruins machinery.

"The crops are long since ruined. . . . Fifteen feet down, the ground is dry as dust. Trees are dying by the thousands. Cattle and horses are dying, some from starvation and some from dirt they eat on the grass. . . . Newspapers say the deaths of many babies and old people are attributed to breathing in so much dirt."

Anne Marie Low recalled her teenage years on a North Dakota farm in her book *Dust Bowl Diary* (1984).

percent of the nation. By the thousands, farm families abandoned their lands and headed west to California. Called "Okies" (because so many Oklahoma families moved), these migrant workers were so numerous that California officials posted guards at state borders to keep out people they considered undesirable.

THE AMERICAN WAY

The federal government took little action on behalf of Depression-crushed citizens. President Herbert Hoover optimistically told the public that the nation was still okay. Hoover believed in what became known as "rugged individualism," but his approving contemporaries called it "the American way." To them, the Amercian way meant:
1. No government aid should be given to "special interests" such as workers and farmers.
2. No government restrictions should be put on business activities.

3. Government legislation about business should help, not harm, competition.

Hoover did not want to spend money on economic relief. He did want to balance the federal budget. Late in his presidency, Hoover approved government loans to states to create local programs that would aid unemployed workers and farmers. But he remained totally opposed to any direct economic relief to

Below: *A migrant family walks on the highway from Idabel to Krebs, Oklahoma, in search of work.*

Above: *A Hooverville in Seattle, Washington, shown here in 1937, was one of many such communities for the homeless created by unemployed workers during the Great Depression.*

> "When the Republican Party came into full power, it went at once resolutely back to our fundamental conception of the state and the rights and responsibilities of the individual. Thereby it restored confidence and hope in the American people, it freed and stimulated enterprise, it restored the government to its position as an umpire instead of a player in the economic game. . . . Economic freedom cannot be sacrificed if political freedom is to be preserved. Even if Government conduct of business could give us more efficiency instead of less efficiency, the fundamental objection to it would remain unaltered. . . . It would destroy political equality. . . . Government operation and control . . . would strike at the very roots of American life and would destroy the very basis of American progress. Our people have the right to know whether we can continue to solve our great problems without abandonment of our American system. I know we can."

Speech by Herbert Hoover, October 22, 1928. During that year's presidential campaign, he set forth his basic belief in individual responsibility and his opposition to a government-directed society.

TIME LINE
1931

The first dust storms begin in reaction to severe drought in Midwestern and Great Plains states; fourteen dust storms will sweep across the Great Plains in 1932, with thirty-eight more in 1933.

President Hoover explains his firm belief that the federal government should leave unemployment relief and farm aid to private charities and local government or risk destroying the American spirit of personal responsibility and individual generosity.

Above: *A wall of dust approaching a Kansas town, 1935.*

individuals, federal regulation of business activity, and all large-scale public works projects. His belief in the principles of "the American way" forbade such actions.

AN ARMY INVADES WASHINGTON, D.C.

In spring of 1932, a small group of unemployed World War I veterans left Portland, Oregon, on a cross-country march to Washington, D.C. They intended to demand cash bonuses for their service, as was promised to them by the U.S. Congress in 1924. Payment was not due until 1945, but the needy veterans wanted their money now. Along the way, others joined the group until fifteen to twenty thousand marchers entered the capital city in May. The Bonus Expeditionary Force, or, as the newspapers called them, the "Bonus Army," set up camp in tents or hastily erected shelters made of packing crates and old lumber, on rough ground across the Potomac River from the Capitol. For the next two months, the peaceful "army" waited in vain to receive their payments. In late July, following a few skirmishes between veterans and police, an angry president ordered

Above: *General MacArthur led army troops against Bonus Marchers in the capital.*

federal soldiers to clear the camps. Troops commanded by General Douglas MacArthur and assisted by Major Dwight D. Eisenhower defeated veterans and their families and torched their shelters. Americans, who were already disgusted with Hoover, thought this was his most shameful blunder.

THE CAMPAIGN OF CHANGE

In 1932, there was little doubt that the Republicans, the party in power, were in deep trouble.

Many resented Hoover, and most believed that if he was reelected, he would continue with the same policies that had already proved useless in solving the nation's problems. However, voters had good reasons to doubt whether his challenger, Democrat Franklin D. Roosevelt (FDR), would do a better job. During the campaign, FDR confused the public about what he believed and what he would do as president. He labeled Hoover as a

Below: *Bonus Marchers are removed from their camp by the United States Army.*

"President Hoover issued orders to the police to . . . clear Pennsylvania Avenue. . . . The demonstrators were quickly dispersed, three of their leaders being arrested. . . . In my judgment, there was not the slightest possibility of any really serious trouble developing, for there is in these bonus-seekers no revolt, no fire, not even smoldering resentment. Who are the bonus-seekers? They are mostly farmworkers, fruit pickers, itinerant factory workers, and other unskilled or semi-skilled laborers. . . . A large minority of the men are skilled mechanics, white-collar workers, and even professional people. . . . Every one of them has been thoroughly whipped by his individual economic circumstances. There is about the lot of them an atmosphere of hopelessness, of utter despair . . . [with] no stomach for fighting. There is no doubt that Washington officialdom from Mr. Hoover on down is badly frightened by the presence of these former soldiers."

Writer Mauritz A. Hallgren, in *The Nation*, July 27, 1932, captured the character and mood of the Bonus Army marchers.

"big spender," but he promised financial help to every troubled group in the nation. Nevertheless, Americans were fed up with Hoover. Roosevelt won with more than 57 percent of the popular vote. The public wanted a strong, decisive leader. They got their wish. In his first Inaugural Address, March 4, 1933, President Roosevelt tried to raise the hopes of the people. He promised quick government action to solve problems.

Below: *Franklin D. Roosevelt won the 1932 presidential election with 57 percent of the popular vote.*

Above: *Major Dwight D. Eisenhower assisted General MacArthur in clearing the Bonus Army camp.*

TIME LINE 1932–1933

MAY 1932
More than three hundred World War I veterans leave Portland, Oregon, on an eighteen-day trip across the United States to urge Congress to pass a Bonus Bill.

OCTOBER 1933
The largest agricultural strike in U.S. history begins in California's San Joaquin Valley among thousands of workers who had fled the Dust Bowl seeking work.

MARCH 1933
New president Roosevelt declares that banks will close while regulators check that they are sound. Three days later, Congress passes the Emergency Banking Act.

"So, first of all, let me assert my firm belief that the only thing we have to fear is fear itself—nameless, unreasoning, unjustified terror, which paralyzes needed efforts to convert retreat into advance. . . . This nation asks for action, and action now. . . . Our greatest primary task is to put people to work. . . . It can be accomplished in part by direct recruiting by the Government itself, treating the task as we would treat the emergency of a war. . . . I am prepared . . . to recommend the measures that a stricken nation in the midst of a stricken world may require. It is to be hoped that the normal balance of executive and legislative authority may be wholly adequate to meet the . . . task before us. . . . But . . . [if necessary] I shall ask the Congress for . . . broad Executive power to wage a war against the emergency."

From Franklin D. Roosevelt's First Inaugural Address, March 4, 1933.

Americans disagreed about whether the new president should make small changes in the current system of government or introduce a new system that greatly strengthened the government's role. Roosevelt's "First New Deal" (1933–1935) stressed economic relief for those in need. A "Second New Deal" (1935–1937) emphasized reform of existing ways. Government programs were patchy in their help for different groups, and some Americans demanded more sweeping changes. Ultimately, despite the best efforts of the government, the New Deal failed.

"The New Deal was a young man's world. . . . . The climate was exciting. . . . You were involved in something that could make a difference. Laws could be changed. So could the conditions of people. . . . Everybody was searching for ideas. A lot of guys were opportunists, some were crackpots. But there was a search, a sense of values. . . . We weren't thinking of remaking society. What was happening was a complete change in social attitudes at the central government level. The question was: How can you do it within this system? FDR was very significant in understanding how best to lead this sort of situation."

Joe Marcus joined the Works Progress Administration in the Spring of 1936.

THE NEW DEALERS

President Roosevelt brought a close circle of advisers (known as the "brain trust") to Washington, D.C., including Rexford Tugwell, who helped write many pieces of New Deal legistlation. The New Dealers often disagreed amongst themselves about policies. A few favored a government-run planned economy, although FDR did not. Others wanted the government to force businesses to slow the Great Depression and use regulations to prevent another. Nearly all New Dealers agreed on the necessity of rescuing the U.S. economy through government action.

Roosevelt was happiest when he was busy, and the first one hundred days of his administration were a flurry of activity as he initiated one measure after another. He ended Prohibition, which since 1919 had made the sale of alcohol illegal. He closed down every bank until experts could check to see that

Above: *A group of CCC men prepare to clear bushland in Wolfe County.*

MAY 1933
New Dealers in Congress create a Federal Emergency Relief Administration issuing grants to states of more than $5 million during its first day in action; Congress authorizes establishment of Tennessee Valley Authority.

OCTOBER 1933
New Dealers establish the Civil Works Administration (CWA) to employ up to four million people to build new schools, hospitals, airports, playgrounds, parks, and bridges.

1934
Lawyer and judge Florence E. Allen becomes the first woman to serve as a federal justice.

their records were in order. Within one month, 75 percent of the banks were open again, and the banking system began to prosper because the public believed the president. In a bid to help farmers, Roosevelt set up the Agricultural Adjustment Administration (AAA), which paid them not to grow crops. This raised the price of the crops they did grow. To attack unemployment, a number of federal government agencies were founded. The Civilian Conservation Corps (CCC) employed young men between the ages of seventeen and twenty-seven (eventually about five hundred thousand total) in conservation efforts across the nation.

INDUSTRIAL RECOVERY AND RURAL ELECTRICITY

Two new programs stood out for their boldness and the controversy they sparked. The National Industrial Recovery Act created two new agencies to help reduce unemployment. The Public Works Administration (PWA) pumped billions of dollars into public works such as bridges, tunnels, and harbors. The National Recovery Administration (NRA) had the government work with industries to draft voluntary agreements (codes) to control wages and prices. The government also supported the labor unions' right to bargain with employers about wages and hours.

"The NRA . . . was one of the most successful things the New Deal did. It was killed when it should have been killed. But when it was created, American business was completely demoralized. Violent price cutting and wage cutting . . . nobody could make any plans for tomorrow. . . . The NRA revived belief that something could be done. It set a floor on prices and on wages.

Pressures had been coming from business to get free of anti-trust acts and have business run business. Pressure was coming from labor for a shorter work week to spread jobs. . . . The Government had a role to play in industrial activity. . . . In the two years of the NRA, the index of industrial production went up remarkably. . . . More than anything else, the NRA changed the climate. It served its purpose."

Gardiner C. Means reflected on working with the National Recovery Administration.

Above: *The Blue Eagle was the symbol of the NRA.*

Critics cursed the NRA for putting private businesses under government control. The U.S. Supreme Court eventually declared the NRA unconstitutional (illegal).

Equally ambitious, but far more successful, was the establishment of the Tennessee Valley Authority (TVA). In Tennessee and six other poverty-stricken southern states, the government employed thousands of workers to build dams throughout the Tennessee River basin. These dams controlled flooding, improved navigation, and made electricity from the force of the water. This brought inexpensive electric power to farms and small towns across the region for the first time. TVA opponents said that government should not compete with private utility companies.

MINORITIES IN THE NEW DEAL

Although the president and many New Dealers talked about the "forgotten man," this usually meant a white man. Mexican-Americans got little government help. Many labored as migrant farm workers, ignored by most New Deal programs.

At the time, American Indians had the least education, the shortest life-spans, and the highest child death rate of all Americans. The goverment recognized that there was a concern and created a new Indian Reorganization Act, but it accomplished little, although some tribes acquired more land, and the number of American Indians employed by the government increased.

> "If I was to vote today, I'd vote for Roosevelt. I don't care if he is a Democrat, he helps the poor man and the farmer. They say that Hoover told 'em over the radio that the jobs should be given to the whites and the colored people could go rabbit-hunting. People can't live on rabbits. . . . I honors Lincoln for freein' us. But the Republican party has changed. . . . [It] stands for the rich man. . . . Roosevelt is for all the poor folks, white and black. . . . Some of the colored people tries to hide it that they's votin' for Roosevelt. . . . But I talks for him and I don't care if I do get scolded for it."

Virgil Johnson, a poor black North Carolina farmer, 1938.

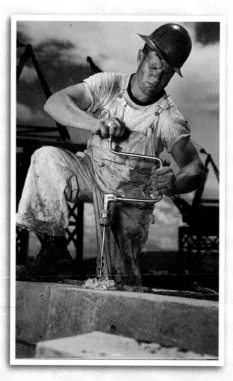

African Americans benefited some. Eleanor Roosevelt, wife of the president, championed the rights of African Americans far more than her husband did. FDR did end racial segregation in federal employment, and other New Dealers set up job training programs. Unfair treatment, however, limited the efforts of blacks to find work. Many New Deal programs gave local governments, in which racism ruled, the authority to spend federal relief dollars. Despite this, African Americans strongly supported FDR as the first president since Abraham Lincoln to work on their behalf.

Left: *A carpenter at work on Douglas Dam, Tennessee, for the TVA.*

SIMPLE SOLUTIONS FOR SERIOUS PROBLEMS

Revolution seemed a real possibility to many Americans during the 1930s. Labor strikes and violence swept city streets. Voices of protest grew louder. Membership of the American Communist Party rose. A California candidate for governor received nearly one million votes on a plan that called for the unemployed to seize idle factories and lands from businesses. Dr. Francis Townsend, a retired physician, said recovery would happen if all citizens over the age of sixty quit their jobs, accepted $200 a month from the government, and spent it in thirty days. Senator Huey P. Long presented the simplest and most radical plan to redistribute the nation's wealth. He wanted families to receive annual incomes and the government to give each family enough money to buy a house and an automobile.

THE SECOND NEW DEAL, 1935–1937

Pressed by protesters, FDR pushed reforms that New Dealers hoped would prevent another depression in the future. A new Works Progress Administration (WPA) put workers, eventually more than eight million of them, directly on the federal payroll. In addition to public works projects, the WPA employed writers, actors, artists, and musicians. Although critics

Left: *Poor black farmers, such as this woman from Texas, were championed by both FDR and his wife Eleanor.*

TIME LINE 1934–1935

1934
With 260 million acres of farm land stripped by dust storms, Congress passes the Frazier-Lemke Farm Bankruptcy Act, allowing the federal government to restrict banks' ability to take away farmers' homes and lands.

1935
On April 14, known as "Black Sunday," the worst dust storm of the Dust Bowl era brings severe damage in several states.

1935
FDR creates the Works Progress Administration (WPA), employing millions across the nation.

"The whole line of my political thought has always been that America must face the time when the whole country would shoulder the obligation, which it owes to every child born on earth—that is a fair chance to life, liberty, and happiness. . . . It was after my disappointment over the Roosevelt policy . . . that I saw the light. I soon began to understand that, regardless of what we had been promised, our only chance . . . was to organize the men and women of the United States so that they were a force capable of action. . . . We are calling upon the people of America, upon the men and women who love this country and who would save their children and their neighbors from calamity and distress. . . . Lincoln freed the black man, but today the white and the black are shackled far worse than any colored person in 1860."

In a 1935 "Letter to Members of the Share Our Wealth Society," Huey Long criticized FDR, outlined his own plan to redistribute wealth, and hinted at revolutionary action.

called WPA workers "lazy bums on the federal dole" (government handouts), the agency benefited communities across the nation. New Dealers approved the Wagner Act, which required employers to bargain fairly with labor unions. A new Banking Act increased federal control over banks. Another action, called the "Soak-the-Rich Tax," raised taxes on incomes of more than $50,000 a year. The Social Security Act stood as the centerpiece of the New Deal. It created a system of old age pensions, unemployment insurance, and financial assistance to dependent children, the blind, the deaf, and people with disabilities. The federal government directly paid old age pensions; the states distributed all other benefits. Both employers and employees paid taxes to support the program. Social Security remains vital in U.S. society today.

THE NEW DEAL FALLS APART

From 1937 on, the New Deal began to die a slow death. FDR lost some of his political magic when he proposed a "court packing" scheme. It aimed to replace elderly members of the Supreme Court who had opposed New Deal measures with judges who were more friendly to his reforms. Next, Roosevelt responded to loud cries against the growing national debt by ordering sharp cutbacks in spending, especially in farm supports and of WPA funds. The result was a sudden fall in farm prices and a sharp increase in unemployment. People called this the "Roosevelt Recession" in the midst of the ongoing Great Depression.

Above: *Two pledges made by the federal government to the people of the United States, promising to aid dependent children and to help the blind.*

TO AID THE NEEDY BLIND

TO AID DEPENDENT CHILDREN

So that dependent children can grow up in their own families, the Federal Government and the States provide cash allowances.

More children will thus have a chance to live normal, wholesome lives in their own homes.

SOCIAL SECURITY BOARD

"By the time the study [of social security legislation] was fully launched, the president's imaginative mind had begun to play over it. . . . He would say . . . I see no reason why every child, from the day he is born, shouldn't be a member of the social security system. When he begins to grow up, he should know he will have old-age benefits direct from the insurance system to which he will belong all his life. If he is out of work, he gets a benefit. If he is sick or crippled, he gets a benefit. . . . Everybody ought to be in on it; the farmer and his wife and his family. 'I don't see why not,' he would say, as across the table, I began to shake my head. 'I don't see why not. From the cradle to the grave they ought to be in a social insurance system.'"

In *The Roosevelt I Knew* (1946), Francis Perkins, who helped to shape social security, remembered how President Roosevelt expressed his bold ideas about universal *coverage*

Above: *A photograph of some WPA workers in 1938. They were employed to pave drainage ditches.*

TIME LINE 1935–1936

1935
In August, the Social Security Act established government responsibility for the social welfare of millions.

1936
Violent labor strikes rock the nation; Huey Long organizes Share Our Wealth Society.

Bitterness was directed at the president from many sides. Numerous business leaders had long since despised Roosevelt. A new alliance of southern Democrats and northern Republicans in Congress increasingly refused to pass additional New Deal laws. Even some of the president's earliest "brain trusts" turned against him. They believed that Roosevelt had gone too far down the road of building "big government" in the United States.

Left: *Two musicians employed by the WPA take a break during a performance in Texas during 1935.*

ONCE UPON A TIME

Above: *Poster created as part of the arts development of the Second New Deal.*

"The first New Deal was a radical departure from American life. It put more power in the central Government. At the time, it was necessary. . . . We merely needed to get the farms prospering again and create a market for the industrial products in the cities. The second New Deal was an entirely different thing. . . . Roosevelt didn't follow any particular policy after 1936. I think he was tired of reform. He began to bring in the radical elements. . . . Business went along with him in his early reforms, but after 1937, it began to be nervous about where he was going. He was improvising all the time. Hit or miss. . . . I said welfare is a narcotic [a drug], because it will never end. . . . The Government can't put people to work. . . . Finally . . . I quit. I never went back to him again."

Raymond Moley, leader of FDR's original "brain trust," abandoned the president in 1936. Shortly thereafter, he wrote a highly critical book, *After Seven Years* (1939), about Roosevelt.

CHAPTER 4

CLIMAX AND AFTERMATH A WARTIME ECONOMY

Above: *Ordinary Americans campaign for funds to help the Allies win the war.*

The United States was not alone in its economic woes. The Great Depression was a worldwide phenomenon, as most of the leading economies suffered severe down-turns in fortunes. In Europe, the Soviet Union, and Japan, harsh dictatorships rose in response to economic struggles. As a result of the actions of Germany's Adolf Hitler, war erupted in Europe in 1939. Although the United States was reluctant to become directly involved in the war initially, it was the U.S. entry into the conflict in late 1941 that finally resolved the many problems posed by the Great Depression.

EUROPE SPINNING ON AN AXIS

The world beyond the borders of the United States became increasingly unstable during the 1930s. Led by Adolf Hitler, Germany created a power-hungry government and promised to unite all Germans, wherever they lived in Europe, into one nation. In Italy, Benito Mussolini used terrorism and murder to erect a single-party state with himself as dictator. About the same time, in Asia, a Japanese military government invaded China and pledged to expand Japan's empire quickly. In 1937, the three nations together created an Axis (group of cooperating countries) of power that terrified Europe. War appeared inevitable. An alarmed President Roosevelt wanted to take action against what he called the "bandit nations." Many Americans, however, opposed involvement with world affairs. Congress passed three Neutrality Acts designed to keep the United States out of war. Numerous U.S. leaders urged the president to continue to fight the Great

> "Never before . . . has our American civilization been in such danger as now. . . . The Nazi masters of Germany have made it clear that they intend not only to dominate all life and thought in their own country, but also to enslave the whole of Europe, and then to use the resources of Europe to dominate the rest of the world. . . . [We must send] every ounce and every ton of munitions and supplies that we can possibly spare to help the defenders who are in the front lines. . . . We must be the great arsenal of democracy."
>
> **President Franklin D. Roosevelt delivered a "fireside chat" on radio, December 29, 1940, to inform the world that the United States would help other nations at war with the Axis.**

Depression instead of focusing on international troubles.

PEARL HARBOR

By summer 1941, relations between Japan and the United States had fallen apart. Controlling China and French Indochina (Vietnam today), Japan was poised to take over all of Southeast Asia. Roosevelt stopped all U.S. trade with Japan and forbade access to Japanese money invested in U.S. banks. Japanese leaders pressured the United States to accept their dominance in Asia. The United States responded that Japan had to leave China and abandon the Axis. While continuing diplomacy, Japan secretly prepared to attack U.S. forces in the Pacific Ocean region. Early on Sunday, December 7, 1941, Japanese airplanes bombed and battered the U.S. Pacific Fleet of ships anchored in Pearl Harbor, Hawaii. On December

Above: *The rise to power of Adolf Hitler and the Nazis plunged the world into war.*

8, Roosevelt told a shocked nation that the previous day was "a date that will live in infamy," and he asked Congress to declare war on Japan. A reluctant United States was at war. Three days later, honoring their Axis agreement, Germany and Italy declared war on the United States.

Left: *A scene of destruction at Pearl Harbor after the Japanese attack during December 1941.*

TIME LINE
1937–1942

1937
Start of the Shelterbelt Project—to prevent further soil erosion.

1939
Abundant rain ends nearly nine years of drought; within a few years, the Great Plains states were again fertile.

1941
Japan's attack on Pearl Harbor, Hawaii, on December 7 brings the United States fully into World War II.

1942
Responding to fears about Japanese Americans acting as spies, Roosevelt signs Executive Order 9066. This suspends their civil rights, takes away homes and businesses worth more than $500 million, and establishes ten concentration camps in remote sections of the country.

"And now that we are in this war, why I think we should really go all out. . . . And I think that we should forget everything, all fun, all everything and get in the serious business of sure enough winning the war. Let's draft not only just people, let's take money and factories, and men, and women, and kids, everything. . . . And so I think if a man just loses part of his money, why, he can make that back. If he loses all of it, he can make that back, too. . . . I say let's quit all the foolishness and go out and win the war. After all, this country's just a big family, and it's being threatened by a bunch of dictators."

Jack Carlyle, who lived near Fairville, Arkansas, gave his opinion to President Roosevelt in this "Man in the Street" interview in January 1942. His comments showed how quick average Americans were to put the Great Depression behind them for the purpose of national unity.

Above: *A cover from the Saturday Evening Post lauding the contribution of "Rosie the Riveter."*

Above: *A poster urging every American to make a direct contribution to the war effort.*

FULL EMPLOYMENT AT LAST

All the New Deal programs put together did not solve the Depression's major problems—unemployment and the greatly unequal distribution of income. War production did, however. In 1940, unemployment was about seven million. By 1944, almost full employment had returned. Employers hired every person that would work, including retired Americans, minorities, disabled people, and children (about three million, ages twelve to seventeen). By war's end, the average income was double what it had been in 1939. Personal savings soared. Lower-income Americans received a larger percentage of national income than ever before. The largest group of the newly employed was women. Traditionally told they should stay at home, during the war about 6.5 million women, more than half for the

Above: *Inexpensive housing built by the government to rehouse people migrating to the cities during the 1940s.*

first time, went to work. Although women did various jobs, many worked in factories for higher pay. Women took on jobs earlier reserved for men. A famous symbol of the female factory worker was "Rosie the Riveter."

SOLVING THE HOUSING PROBLEM

During the Great Depression, New Dealers tried to ease housing shortages with federal funds for private and public housing construction. Their efforts were not very successful. In the early 1940s, about one million people moved to cities to take jobs in the defense industries. Their migration worsened an already critical need for housing. At war's end, there were few newly built homes for sale or

"I worked the graveyard shift 12:00–8:00 A.M., in the shipyard. I took classes on how to weld. I had leather gloves, leather pants, big hood, goggles, and a leather jacket. . . . We held the welding rod with one hand and the torch fire in the right hand. They put me forty feet down in the bottom of the ship to be a tacker. I filled the long seams of the cracks in the ship corners full of hot lead and then brushed them good and you could see how pretty it was. The welders would come along and weld it so it would take the strong waves and deep water and heavy weight. I liked it pretty good. Lots of people came to Richmond to work in the shipyards. Lots of women went to work to help with the war. I told Melvin later that I helped to make a ship for him to come home in."

Katie Melvin told of her experiences in moving from Oklahoma to California with her husband and baby; her husband joined the Marines while Katie went to work in a Richmond, California, factory.

Above: *Hispanic children outside a company housing settlement in New Mexico.*

A1943
Racial conflict explodes with about 274 riots in almost fifty cities that are centers of wartime production and have integrated apartment projects.

1944
General Motors executive Charles E. Wilson, speaking for the War Production Board, proposes a post-war "permanent war economy," in which major corporations and the military will work hand in hand; this is the origin of the "military-industrial complex."

1944
Supreme Court, in Korematsu v. U.S., upholds Japanese relocation on grounds of national security; Roosevelt creates the War Refugee Board to aid refugees, mostly European Jews; FDR elected to fourth term in office.

apartments for rent. But both the federal government and private businesses did build "temporary" housing for workers in war industries. That action expanded the earlier principle of government provision of housing. Several years after the war, Congress passed the Housing Act of 1949 that firmly committed the federal government to

financial support of housing construction. Perhaps the most interesting examples of temporary wartime housing were the many privately owned and government-provided "trailer camps" that sprang up around the nation.

Left: *A worker operates a hand drill in the process of assembling a fighter plane.*

"Across the length and breadth of America at war can be seen compact colonies of strange little cottages on wheels . . . known as trailers . . . They are used to house workers in American war industries and other plants, which have sprung up like giant mushrooms all over the United States. . . . People do not live in trailers because they like the idea of being [travelers], but generally because there are few houses to rent in the big war industry centers. There are many big government trailer camps, which often have excellent facilities to offer the tenants. One I lived in had 3,000 people, nearly 1,000 of them children. . . . War has caused such enormous migrations . . . that it is hard for the mind to compass. From the north to the south, people have left their familiar surroundings, the comforts of their homes and gone to work in munition centers, in aircraft plants, or shipbuilding yards."

Mary Heaton Vorse, a well-known investigator of the nation's housing problems, traveled around the United States during the war, living for short periods in the different kinds of trailer colonies that she described in her article *U.S. Trailer Camps*.

Above: Many people empathized with this tale of a poor family's struggle.

Above: The popular ventriloquist Edgar Bergen and dummy Charlie McCarthy.

Novels, stories, plays, songs, comic books, movies, and other pieces of popular culture often tell us about people. People's fears, hopes, and the events of their daily lives are expressed in the kinds of materials they listened to, read, or watch. Entertainment also helped people to cope with the misery of the Great Depression because it helped them to forget about their troubles for a short time.

BROTHER, CAN YOU SPARE A DIME?

Popular songs mirrored changes in the public's mood as the Great Depression deepened. In 1930, hopeful Americans sang "Happy Days Are Here Again." The next year, as national income fell more than 30 percent, the less optimistic song, "I've Got Five Dollars," played repeatedly on radio. By 1932, the Depression had cut national income to less than half its worth at the time of the crash. That year's popular song was quite grim: "Brother, Can You Spare A Dime?" More than any other popular song, this showed the feelings of many forgotten and unemployed Americans. Those who could afford it flocked to see the Broadway play *Tobacco Road*. This realistic but gloomy account of southern rural poverty ran throughout the Depression, from 1933 to 1941, setting all-time attendance records. John Steinbeck's classic novel *The Grapes of Wrath* (1939) portrayed the powerless versus the powerful in its story of one Dust Bowl farm family fleeing Oklahoma for a supposed better life in California, but failing. The appearance of the new comic book *Superman* in

"They used to tell me I was building a dream, and so I followed the mob,
When there was earth to plow, or guns to bear, I was always there right on the job.
They used to tell me I was building a dream, with peace and glory ahead,
Why should I be standing in line, just waiting for bread?
Once I built a railroad, I made it run, made it race against time.
Once I built a railroad; now it's done. Brother, can you spare a dime?
Once I built a tower, up to the sun, brick, and rivet, and lime;
Once I built a tower, now it's done. Brother, can you spare a dime?
Once in khaki suits, gee we looked swell,
Full of that Yankee Doodly Dum,
Half a million boots went slogging through Hell,
And I was the kid with the drum!
Say, don't you remember, they called me Al; it was Al all the time.
Why don't you remember, I'm your pal? Buddy, can you spare a dime?"

🎵   **"Brother, Can You Spare A Dime" (lyrics by Yip Harburg,
music by Gorney Harburg), 1931**

1938 perhaps underlined the public's desire for a hero to help solve their problems.

VARIETY IS THE SPICE OF LIFE

Radio shows were the most popular form of entertainment in the 1930s. Listeners thrilled to adventures such as *The Lone Ranger* and *The Green Hornet,* in which masked heroes brought justice to those causing troubles. Even more popular were variety shows featuring comedians such as Jack Benny, Fred Allen, George Burns, Gracie Allen, and ventriloquist Edgar Bergen with his dummy Charlie McCarthy. Orchestras and singers performed at spots during the programs. One popular show, *Fibber McGee and Molly,* was about a dim-witted husband and shrewd wife trying to get by on a modest income. The script excerpt (included in this chapter) from the long-running radio program

Above: *The enduring comic Superman reflected Depression-era people's search for a superhero to solve their woes.*

Left: *The Lone Ranger (right) and Tonto from the popular television series that ran between 1949 and 1957.*

TIME LINE 1945–1946

1945
FDR dies and vice-president Harry S Truman takes over; Germany surrenders; first atomic bombs dropped on Hiroshima and Nagasaki; Japan surrenders, ending World War II.

1945
Crisis in Iran and civil war in Greece bring the United States and the Soviet Union into the first direct "Cold War" conflict.

1946
Republican congressional victories mark end of New Deal coalitions, hampering passage of additional New Deal-type legislation.

FIBBER McGEE AND MOLLY Tuesday April 18, 1939: "Molly Wants a Budget"

HARLOW (the announcer): Well, folks, as you all know by now, Molly is home again, and after looking over the household bills . . .

MOLLY: McGee, look at this milk bill! What on earth you been doin'? Sprinklin' the lawn with it?

FIBBER: (Sheepishly) It is a little high, ain't it? What say we get a cow?

MOLLY: Who's gonna milk it?

FIBBER: Oh, you gotta milk 'em?

MOLLY: No, you just leave some empty bottles around the barn and then go out in the morning and rob the cow's nest. Do you have to milk 'em?!? And how 'bout this electric light bill?

FIBBER: Ooh, is that high, too?

MOLLY: Is it high? Well, look at it. Looks like the annual report of the TVA.

MOLLY: Look at this telephone bill.

FIBBER: Huh?

MOLLY: Thirty-four dollars! Can't Europe settle its own problems? Did you have to call 'em up and give 'em advice?

> "In depression movies, traditional beliefs in the possibilities of individual success are kept alive in the early thirties under various guises. . . . Hollywood would help the nation's fundamental institutions escape unscathed by attempting to keep alive the myth and wonderful fantasy of a mobile and classless society, by focusing on the endless possibilities for individual success, by turning social evil into personal evil and making the New Deal into a . . . leading man."

Historian Andrew Bergman on the social significance of movies in his book, *We're in the Money: Depression America and Its Films* (1971).

Above: *A poster from the Hollywood blockbuster Gone with the Wind.*

Above: *The heroes of pulp fiction filled people's needs for a hero to rescue them.*

illustrates how variety show comedians often used references to current events as part of their humor.

OFF TO WORK WE GO

Sixty to seventy-five million Americans attended movies each week during the 1930s. Movie studios cut ticket prices and introduced gimmicks such as "Bank Night" (when cash prizes were given to lucky ticket holders) and "Crockery Night" (when inexpensive china was given away). Gangster films, musicals, westerns,

comedies, and government agent movies flashed across the screen. Walt Disney released the first animated feature film, *Snow White and the Seven Dwarfs,* in 1937. The blockbuster color film *Gone with the Wind,* about the American Civil War, captured audiences two years later. Americans also flocked to theaters to view "topical" films that dealt realistically with current social life. *I Am a Fugitive From a Chain Gang* (about a wronged man in a

Above: *A still from Disney's first feature animation film,* Snow White and the Seven Dwarfs, *a release from the grimness of many people's ordinary lives.*

TIME LINE
1947–1948

1947
Truman Doctrine promises to challenge Communism throughout the world; Secretary of State George C. Marshall announces European Recovery Plan (Marshall Plan); National Security Act creates new Department of Defense; Republicans push through Taft-Hartley Act in effort to cripple power of labor unions.

1948
Harry S Truman defeats Republican presidential candidate Thomas E. Dewey, showing that New Deal reform spirit, although heavily attacked, has some life left.

southern prison) and *Wild Boys of the Road* (teenagers riding the rails and living in "Hoovervilles"), among other films, addressed the problems that many Depression-era citizens faced.

BEATING TO A PULP

A new kind of magazine appeared in the 1930s—the pulp magazine (stories printed on paper made from crushing wood, old paper, and rags). "Pulp fiction" was a term given to sensational adventure stories, featuring mysterious heroes who fought battles against crime and injustice. Colorful and often shocking covers tempted readers. Because of their exciting stories and cheap price, pulp magazines became enormously popular with a mass reading public. Unlike many popular songs, plays, novels, and movies that were about everyday life, pulp fiction offered a kind of escape from the daily problems of the Great Depression. The first pulp magazine, *The Shadow: A Detective Story*, reached the newsstands in 1931.

Left: *Clark Gable and Claudette Colbert are shown here finding love against the odds in the 1934 film,* It Happened One Night.

"Steve Cronin's fear-glazed eyes distinguished the outline of a black cloak with a broad-brimmed black hat that seemed to merge with the form beneath. From between the hat and the cloak glared two eyes that shone like beads of fire! Then came the voice—a low, ghostly voice. . . . 'Steve Cronin,' it said. 'I am The Shadow.' Silence. The crook could not move. . . . 'Steve Cronin,' said the voice of The Shadow. 'I have watched you. . . . One time more will be the last. That is my warning. Three times will mean your doom.' The figure seemed to dwindle as it merged into the darkness. . . . Steve Cronin's limbs gained a sudden strength of frenzied fear. A low, gasping scream escaped his lips as he yanked the door open and half flung himself into the hall. A sound followed him from the room—it was a mirthless, mocking laugh!"

Maxwell Grant (pen name for Walter Gibson) wrote more than 280 stories between 1931 and 1949 in which the Shadow defeated evil scientists, criminals, and foreign invaders (during World War II). This extract is from *Eyes of the Shadow.*

The New Deal's response to the Great Depression permanently changed U.S. society. Instead of expecting to be wholly responsible for themselves, citizens looked to Washington, D.C., expecting the federal government to be part of their daily lives. Government involvement became critical to the economy. Foreign and domestic policies rode the backs of New Deal actions. Politics pivoted on support or opposition to New Deal-type reforms.

Above: *The arrival of atomic weapons ushered in the Cold War, a political state that would dominate the world for decades.*

MILITARY INDUSTRIAL COMPLEX

After World War II, Depression-scarred Americans feared another economic collapse. Businesspeople worried that the end of production for war supplies would mean hard times. Workers worried their jobs would disappear. Fears dissolved in a postwar economic boom. Tired of sacrifices and supported by high wartime wages and growing savings accounts, consumers bought all kinds of long-unavailable goods. Government spending played an equally important role. The GI Bill (1944) erected a welfare program for war veterans that

"Until the latest of our world conflicts, the United States had no armaments industry. American makers of plowshares could, with time and as required, make swords as well. But now we can no longer risk emergency improvisation of national defense; we have been compelled to create a permanent armaments industry of vast proportions. Added to this, three and one-half million men and women are directly engaged in the defense establishment. We annually spend on military security more than the net income of all United States corporations. This conjunction of an immense military establishment and a large arms industry is new in the American experience. The total influence economic, political, even spiritual is felt in every city, every State house, every office of the Federal government. We . . . must not fail to comprehend its grave implications. . . . In the councils of government, we must guard against the acquisition of unwarranted influence, whether sought or unsought, by the military-industrial complex."

President Dwight D. Eisenhower recognized the enormous impact of government spending on the economy, yet he warned his fellow citizens about possible future problems in his "Farewell Address" in January, 1961.

paid for health care, education, and housing, while also pouring millions of dollars into the economy. Even more significant was a massive rise in military spending. Industrial leaders and government officials discovered they shared a mutual interest— businesspeople wanted to make profits while politicians wanted a reliable national defense. The result was what came to be known as the "military-industrial complex." Defense projects kept businesses going and the post-war economy humming. It would continue to do so into the twenty-first century.

THE COLD WAR AND THE NEW DEAL

The term "Cold War" was coined by U.S. economist and presidential adviser Bernard Baruch. It refers to the hostile relationship between the United States and the Soviet Union, and their respective allies, following the end of World War II. During this time, the United States spent billions of dollars on the Marshall Plan, or European Recovery Program, which was a humanitarian undertaking to provide economic aid to war-torn Europe. Its architect, U.S. general George C. Marsh, received the

Nobel Peace prize in 1953. The United States also adopted a policy of "containment" toward the Soviet Union. This meant trying to restrict the expansion of the Soviet Union through free trade and, if necessary, military force. The fear of nuclear war following the devastation of Hiroshima and Nagasaki by U.S. bombs helped to avoid military confrontation, but this "Cold War" was to dominate U.S. foreign policy for the next half-century. It was not until the 1970s that moves toward breaking down the barriers formed by years of hostility began.

Left: *Post World War II Europe was split between the capitalist West and communist countries, controlled by the Soviet leader Josef Stalin.*

TIME LINE 1949–1950

1949
Soviet Union tests first atomic bomb; China "falls" to Communists; for Cold War purposes, United States helps shape and joins NATO (North Atlantic Treaty Organization) that pits U.S. and Western European countries against Soviet expansion.

1950
Wisconsin Republican Senator Joseph P. McCarthy gives famous speech in Wheeling, West Virginia, charging that Communists occupy key positions in the Truman administration.

"The man who was middle-aged in 1949 had lived through transformations of life . . . more swift and sweeping than any previous generation of Americans had known. He grew up in a land where free economic enterprise was the normal way. . . . In 1949, this American made his living in a crazy-quilt system. 'New Dealism' people called it all. . . . New Dealism, having labored mightily to lift low-income Americans, found that it had created a nation of the middle class . . . annoyed at . . . placing the values of change above those of standard middle-class thinking. . . . Any irritation with domestic New Dealism was stoked by the Communist threat. . . . Was it not the New Dealers, like the Communists, who talked of uplifting the masses, fighting the businessmen, establishing economic controls over society, questioning the traditional in every part of living?"

Historian Eric F. Goldman in his 1956 book *The Crucial Decade* suggested reasons for enduring opposition to New Deal political and social reforms during the Great Depression.

WiTHOUT THE MARSHALL PLAN

YOUR BREAD WOULD BE BARE......

AND SO WOULD YOUR CHILDREN !

Above: *A poster promoting the virtues of the U.S.-led Marshall Plan, designed to prevent countries falling under the influence of the Soviet Union.*

POST-WAR AFFAIRS

The Depression ushered in the New Deal, which was to promote equality of opportunity, social responsibility, and the general welfare in the United States. In the years that followed, economic growth was accompanied by a huge influx of people. Between 1940 and 1980, an estimated ten million immigrants arrived in the United States. Millions more arrived illegally. Most went to cities that became major centers of economic activity. Service industries expanded as competition, mainly from the European Community (EC) and Japan, ended the United States' industrial predominance. Machines had a huge impact on farming. In 1949, less than 10 percent of the cotton crop was harvested by machine, but by 1969, 96 percent

was. Improved farming methods led to greater yields. Millions of people left southern states for the East, the Midwest, and the West. By 1980, only one-third of the U.S. population lived in rural areas. The economy grew rapidly until the late 1960s, when a period of inflation and deficits was experienced. Economic growth revived in the 1980s and has continued ever since.

THE CORPORATE STATE

Many historians agree that the major domestic legacy of the New Deal was "The Corporate State." By that, they mean a political-economic system of authority shared by several strong groups. Before the Great Depression, big businesses usually had a strong voice in politics. Critics called the United States Senate the "Millionaires' Club." A large majority of cabinet members (government executive officers) for presidents had come directly from heading up large corporations. Because of New Deal

"By and large, and certainly in its primary and steadier movements, the national economy depends not only on systematic price-fixing and noncompetitive bidding but also on the guarantee of government intervention. The theory of the free market works at the margins of the economy among cabdrivers and the owners of pizza parlors . . . but the central pillars of the American enterprise rest firmly on the foundation stones of state subsidy. The federal treasury . . . supplies 45 percent of the nation's income. The politicians . . . trade in every known commodity, and they work the levers of government like gamblers pulling at slot machines. . . ."

Lewis H. Lapham, then editor of the distinguished *Harper's* magazine, explained in a 1990 article, "The Visible Hand," how the American economy actually worked.

Right: *This statue of FDR, along the famous Cherry Tree Walk in Washington, D.C., celebrates his achievements, of which the New Deal looms large.*

Above: *The Capitol in Washington, D.C.*

TIME LINE
1960–1988

1960
President John F. Kennedy promises a "New Frontier" that consists of New Deal-like social and economic programs.

1981–1988
Republican president Ronald Reagan sharply increases military spending, slashes federal spending, and cuts taxes and business regulations.

reforms, however, powers changed. Big businesses shared power with workers in unions and with the federal government. By the last two decades of the twentieth century, labor unions had lost some of their influence, while big businesses and the federal government were so intertwined that some observers couldn't see any separation of powers at all. That was not a result that the New Dealers would have expected or welcomed.

LOOKING TO WASHINGTON

Citizens once looked to city halls or state capitals when they wanted

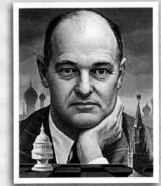

Above: *George Kennan, advocate of the policy of "containment" of the Soviet Union.*

"The Government has still other opportunities; to help raise the standard of living of our citizens . . . social security, health, education, housing, and civil rights."
President Harry S Truman (Democrat), 1949

"We believe that whatever can be done by private effort should be done by private effort rather than by the government—and not the other way round."
President Dwight D. Eisenhower (Republican), 1957

"To help those least fortunate of all, I am recommending a new public welfare program, stressing services instead of support, rehabilitation instead of relief, and training for useful work instead of prolonged dependency."
President John F. Kennedy (Democrat), 1962

> We have lived too long with the consequences of attempting to gather all power and responsibility in Washington. . . . Government must learn to take less from people so that people can do more for themselves."
>
> **President Richard M. Nixon (Republican), 1973**

> "We thought we could transform the country through massive national programs, but often the programs did not work. Too often they only made things worse."
>
> **President Gerald R. Ford (Republican), 1976**

> "We need patience and good will, but we really need to realize that there is a limit to the role and the function of government. Government cannot solve our problems, it can't set our goals, it cannot define our vision."
>
> **President James Earl Carter (Democrat), 1978**

government assistance. Business leaders trumpeted the virtues of free enterprise, which is not shackled by federal government regulations. Conservative voices endorsed personal responsibility and voluntary aid, instead of federal actions, on behalf of individuals who were suffering from economic or family troubles. But the Great Depression showed that many people were not able to make it on their own, and that even big businesses faltered under attack by economic circumstances they could not control. The New Deal firmly established that the federal government would take an ever-larger part in shaping the nation's political, economic, and social affairs. From the 1930s on, the first reaction to troubled times by most Americans began with the question, "What is the president going to do about the situation?"

THE NEW DEAL TODAY

In 1939, President Roosevelt claimed that the New Dealers had crafted "new tools for a new role of government operating in a democracy," and he judged that even "many of those who fought bitterly against the forging of these new tools welcome their use today." He was overly optimistic. Since Franklin D. Roosevelt's presidency, candidates for the office have expressed their opinions either for or against the position taken by the New Deal. Once in office, every president has cast his policy proposals either as logical extensions of the New Deal or as a retreat from its "big government" approach. In that regard, the Great Depression and the New Deal's responses to it remain a vital part of U.S. politics.

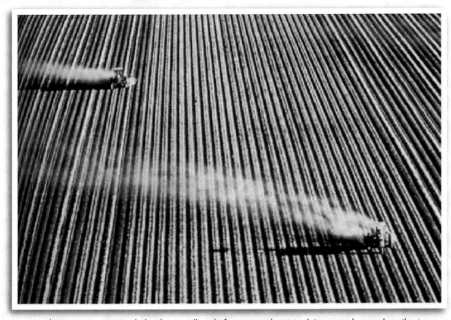

1996
The Personal Responsibility and Work Opportunity Reconciliation Act of 1996 is signed by President Clinton, taking away the guarantee of financial aid to low-income families. The United States' military spending rose to more than that of all the rest of the world combined.

Above: The Great Depression led to less small-scale farming in the United States and toward agribusiness on a large scale.

"But great as our tax burden is, it has not kept pace with public spending. . . . In this present crisis, government is not the solution to our problem."
President Ronald W. Reagan (Republican), 1981

"What government can do alone is limited. . . . We must return to families, communities, counties, cities, states, and institutions of every kind, the power to chart their own destiny. . . ."
President George H.W. Bush (Republican), 1991

"Let us resolve to make our government a place for what Franklin Roosevelt called "bold, persistent exprcimontation," a government of our tomorrows, not our yesterdays. Let us give this capital back to the people to whom it belongs."
President William Jefferson Clinton (Democrat), 1993

". . . we must always remember the goal is to reduce dependency on government and offer every American the dignity of a job."
President George W. Bush (Republican), 2002

Left: President Clinton introduced a series of welfare reforms during his rule that had echoes of the New Deal.

The Great Depression was a turning point in U.S. history. It made people take notice of the inequality that ran through society, from the great divide between rich and poor to the difficulties that affected U.S. citizens of different colors, beliefs, and abilities. After the Depression, welfare programs were put in place to help address these inequalities. Many people helped to shape the United Stated that emerged. These are just some of the key players.

Herbert Hoover (1874–1964)

Many people called Hoover the "Great Engineer" who, through the American Relief Administration, fed most of Europe after World War I. The thirty-first president (1929–1933) responded to the Great Depression by emphasizing voluntary cooperation from businesses rather than government intervention. Determined to promote individual and local responsibility, Hoover rejected direct federal aid for the unemployed and opposed government spending for large public works projects. Through the Reconstruction Finance Corporation (1931) and the Federal Home Loan Bank Act (1932), Hoover offered federal loans to corporations and financial institutions to revive the economy. These actions were too little and too late to help the crisis. By the time he left office, Herbert Hoover was extremely unpopular.

Franklin Delano Roosevelt (1882–1945)

From a background of wealth and privilege, FDR was a reform-minded New York state senator, assistant secretary of the U.S. Navy under President Woodrow Wilson, then Democratic vice-presidential candidate in 1920. Defeating Republican incumbent Herbert Hoover in 1932, FDR promised as president to bring a "New Deal" to the nation. FDR's insistence that government play a strong and active role earned him the hostility of business leaders. Always an internationalist, Roosevelt tried to lead an isolationist public into World War II in 1940. Roosevelt died on April 12, 1945.

Eleanor Roosevelt (1884–1962)

FDR's wife Eleanor became the moral conscience of the New Deal during the 1930s. She was a champion of feminist causes, civil rights, working class Americans, and the immigrant poor. Eleanor exerted tremendous influence through the media and leadership roles in organizations such as the League of Women Voters. After FDR's death (1945), Eleanor became a delegate to the new United Nations. There, she became known as the world's leading human rights advocate, serving as diplomat off and on until her death on November 7, 1962.

Henry A. Wallace (1888–1965)

Iowa-born geneticist, economist, editor, and successful businessman, Wallace served as Secretary of Agriculture (1933–1940) and as vice president (1941–1945). Wallace sparked an agricultural revolution to restore the economic health of farmers, who made up one-quarter of the population in 1933. He fostered soil conservation programs, introduced land-use planning, and promoted research to control plant and animal diseases and to develop hybrid seeds to increase productivity. His innovative government programs sheltered many farmers from the worst ravages of the Great Depression. Although he remained the liberals' darling, Wallace fell from Roosevelt's favor due to his naïve support of the Soviet Union. FDR replaced Wallace with Harry S Truman in the 1944 presidential campaign, a dismissal Wallace never forgave. Wallace ran unsuccessfully for president in 1948 as a candidate for the Progressive Party (a loose coalition of liberal groups).

Rexford Tugwell (1881–1979)

An academic economist, Tugwell was an early member of FDR's "Brain Trust." Suspicious of business leaders, he strongly advocated national government planning. Tugwell helped to write both the Agricultural Adjustment Act and the National Industrial Recovery Act that set up the National Recovery Administration (NRA) of 1933. Tugwell's chief contribution came as head of the Resettlement Administration (1935–1937). He planned, but mostly failed, to move poor farm families to better land. His most ambitious program was government construction of "greenbelt suburbs" near big cities in which to house modest income families. These mostly failed as well. He served as governor of Puerto Rico (1941–1946) then returned to teaching and writing for the remainder of his life.

Harold L. Ickes (1874–1952)

An earlier Chicago Republican reformer, this journalist, lawyer, and writer became a prominent Democrat who supported FDR. He served as Secretary of the Interior (1933–1946) and headed the Public Works Administration (PWA) (1933–1939). Ickes cautiously moved ahead with a massive construction program. Federal government projects not only employed thousands of workers, but they also built 70 percent of the nation's new schools, 65 percent of its city halls and courthouses, and 35 percent of its new hospitals. He irritated fellow officials and angered private business leaders by limiting the power of utility companies and constructing publicly-funded, low-cost competition. Ickes's efforts to clear city slums and replace them with low-cost, government-built housing generated bitter controversy. He set an example for later public housing projects.

Harry Hopkins (1890–1946)

Hopkins headed the Federal Emergency Relief Administration (FERA) (1933–1935). Simultaneously, he was executive of the short-lived Civil Works Administration (CWA) (1933–1934) that employed more than 4.2 million workers. He then led the Works Progress Administration (WPA) (1935–1938), the largest of all the New Deal government agencies. Through various programs, Hopkins distributed more than $8.5 billion dollars in unemployment relief. He clashed frequently with other FDR loyalists, especially Harold Ickes. Hopkins, nonetheless, became the most powerful man in the Roosevelt presidency. Between 1938 and 1940, Hopkins served as Secretary of Commerce. During World War II, he was FDR's closest personal advisor and point man with foreign leaders. The year before his death, Hopkins represented President Truman at the San Francisco conference that established the United Nations.

Frances Perkins (1882–1965)

As the Secretary of Labor, Perkins served longer (1933–1945) than any other member of any presidents' cabinet. Educated as a teacher, her great service to society came as a public official. By the late 1920s, she was well known as a champion of female workers, children, elderly citizens, and the poor in general. President Roosevelt asked her to head his new Committee on Economic Security. It urged national unemployment insurance and old-age insurance to assist the elderly poor. Frances Perkins became one of the architects of the Social Security Act (1935) and worked tirelessly for its passage. After resigning as Secretary of Labor in 1945, public speaking, writing, and teaching about her causes occupied the rest of her life.

John L. Lewis (1880–1969)

From starting work in the coal mines at age sixteen, Lewis rose to the presidency of the United Mine Workers of America (UMWA) in 1920. For the next forty years, Lewis reigned as the nation's most fiery labor leader. A strong advocate of industrial unionism (organizing unskilled and semiskilled workers), Lewis led a break with the powerful American Federation of Labor (that opposed industrial unionism) in the mid-1930s. Lewis helped to create the CIO (Congress of Industrial Organizations) and served as its president (1936–1940). He was ready to call labor strikes to force employers to give benefits to workers. A one-time supporter of FDR, Lewis eventually challenged FDR's domestic and foreign policies and became a Republican in 1940.

Robert F. Wagner (1877–1953)

German-born, Wagner was one of the most influential members of the United States Senate (1927–1949). Wagner imprinted nearly every important piece of New Deal legislation, including the National Industrial Recovery Act (NIRA) (1933) and the Social Security Act (1935). Wagner was the leading champion for government support of labor organizations. The National Labor Relations Act (Wagner Act) of 1935 forced employers to bargain collectively with unions, thereby reversing historic relations between industrialists and workers. His other great triumph was low-cost urban housing. During World War II, Wagner shaped the GI Bill (1944) that benefited returning veterans in educational, housing, and health services. This was one of the most successful governmental planning programs in history.

Felix Frankfurter (1882–1965)

This Austrian-born judge and Harvard Law School professor became a key presidential adviser. Intellectually, he served as a counterpoint to New Dealers who favored centralized government planning through agencies such as the NRA (National Recovery Administration). Frankfurter urged FDR to abandon efforts at business-government cooperation. To return to a more competitive United States, he promoted government regulation of big businesses through anti-trust suits and a taxation of large corporations. Roosevelt named him to the U.S. Supreme Court where he served from 1939 to 1962. He practiced judicial restraint, believing that policies should emerge from legislatures rather from court decisions. He received the Presidential Medal of Freedom for his long career of service to the nation in 1963.

Huey (Pierce) "Kingfish" Long (1893–1935)

"Every Man A King" was the slogan of controversial Louisiana Governor (1928–1932), then United States Senator (1932–1935), Huey Long. Promoting himself as a radical populist (spokesman for common people), Long built a powerful political machine in Louisiana. He emerged as President Roosevelt's major rival. In 1934, Long founded the Share Our Wealth Society. More than twenty-seven thousand local clubs joined his movement. Long promised to eliminate personal fortunes above a certain level and have the federal government guarantee every family an annual income. He warned that without redistribution of wealth, revolution was certain He expected to win the presidency in 1936. He was assassinated by a Louisiana doctor, supposedly opposed to the corrupt methods of the man who called himself the "Kingfish."

address a speech, particularly one given by someone taking office.

armaments means of making war; weapons.

atom bomb a bomb with great destructive power caused by energy released from splitting atoms.

axis an alliance between people, organizations, or countries.

bankruptcy legally-declared inability to pay debts.

bear market a market in which stocks are sold in anticipation of a fall in price.

big government government seen as spending too much and trying to control too many aspects of people's lives.

Black Tuesday the name given to October 29, 1929, the day of the stock market crash.

Bonus Army name given by the newspapers to a group of ex-servicemen who marched on Washington, D.C., in 1932 to ask for bonuses that were promised to them after the end of World War I.

brain trust the name given to a group of skilled advisors brought in by President Franklin Delano Roosevelt when he took office.

bull market a market in which an attempt is made to raise prices by buying large quantities of a particular commodity, thus reducing availability and increasing demand.

CCC Civilian Conservation Corps, a federal government agency that employed young men in conservation efforts across the nation.

Cold War the hostile relations between the former Soviet Union and the United States, and their respective allies, from the end of the World War II to the end of the 1980s.

communist a person who believes in a vision of a classless society in which the state has ownership and control of wealth and property.

concentration camp a prison camp used to hold political prisoners or civilians.

Congress the national legislative body of the United States, consisiting of the House of Representatives and the Senate.

conservation protecting an important environmental or cultural resource from harm, loss, damage, or decay.

cooperative a business that is owned by the people that run it with all profits shared; a group of people working or acting together.

CWA Civil Works Administration; an organization set up in 1933 to employ people to build public projects.

democracy a system of government in which the people as a whole have power, which is usually exercised for them by elected representatives.

Democrat a person who believes in the democratic system of government; a member of the Democratic party.

dictator a person who rules a country with absolute power, usually by force.

drought a period during which there is little or no rainfall.

Dust Bowl an event in which a large area of the United States suffered badly from erosion of the topsoil and wind during the 1930s.

economist a person who is an expert on financial management.

executive a person or body with the power to make decisions and to carry out what is decided.

federal a form of government in which states defer some powers to a central government but retain an element of self-government.

GI Bill a welfare program for war veterans.

Hooverville a shantytown, named after President Herbert Hoover, whom many blamed for failing to halt the downward economic plunge.

inaugural relating to or marking an official beginning.

lodger someone who rents a room in another person's home.

Marshall Plan also known as the European Recovery Plan, a program of humanitarian aid from the United States to postwar Europe.

migration moving from one country or region to another, often in search of work.

mortgage money borrowed over a number of years to buy property on which interest is paid, usually to a bank.

New Deal program of reform introduced in the 1930s under the presidency of Franklin Delano Roosevelt.

NIRA National Industrial Recovery Act, an act that aimed to stimulate economic recovery by meeting the needs of manufacturers and workers.

NRA National Recovery Administration, a body that worked with industry to draft voluntary agreements to control wages and prices.

PWA Public Works Administration, part of the NIRA that carried out useful public works projects and provided jobs.

Republican a member of the political party that favors state and individaul responsibility over federal government involvement.

shanty town a settlement of temporary housing erected using scrap materials by homeless people, usually on the outskirts of a big city.

social security a monetary protection against illness, unemployment, or retirement, usually provided by the government.

speculator a person who makes risky investments of money in the hope of large profits.

stock the capital of a company, divided into shares, or a unit of ownership of a company, consisiting of a group of shares.

TaftHartley Act an act that limited organized labor and changed a number of laws relating to work in a bid to halt strikes.

TVA the Tennessee Valley Authority, a body set up to build dams throughout the Tennessee River basin.

Wall Street a street in New York, the main financial center of the United States.

WPA Works Progress Administration, a federal program that employed people to carry out public works and also employed writers, artists, actors, and musicians.

Please visit our web site at: www.garethstevens.com
For a free color catalog describing Gareth Stevens Publishing's
list of high-quality books and multimedia programs,
call 1-800-542-2595 or 1-800-387-3178 (Canada).
Gareth Stevens Publishing's fax: (414) 332-3567.

Library of Congress Cataloging-in-Publication Data

Schultz, Stanley.
   The Great Depression: a primary source history / Stanley Schultz.
      p. cm. — (In their own words)
   Includes bibliographical references and index.
   ISBN 0-8368-5978-2 (lib. bdg.)
      1. United States—History—1933-1945—Juvenile literature. 2. Depressions—
1929—United States—Juvenile literature. 3. United States—History—1919-1933—
Juvenile literature. 4. United States—History—1933-1945—Sources—Juvenile
literature. 5. Depressions—1929—United States—Sources—Juvenile literature.
6. United States—History—1919-1933—Souces—Juvenile literature. I. Title.
II. In their own words (Milwaukee, Wis.)
   E806.S357   2005
   973.91'6—dc22   2005040893

This North American edition first published in 2006 by
Gareth Stevens Publishing
A Member of the WRC Media Family of Companies
330 West Olive Street, Suite 100
Milwaukee, WI 53212 USA

This U.S. edition copyright © 2006 by Gareth Stevens, Inc.
Original edition copyright © 2005 ticktock Entertainment Ltd.
First published in Great Britain in 2005 by ticktock Media Ltd.,
Unit 2, Orchard Business Centre, North Farm Road, Tunbridge Wells,
Kent, TN2 3XF, U.K.

Gareth Stevens editor: Betsy Rasmussen
Gareth Stevens art direction: Tammy West

Photo credits: (b) bottom; (c) center; (l) left; (r) right; (t) top
Art Archive: 9b, 30-31c, 31t. CORBIS: 1, 5b, 10t, 16-17c, 26t, 26-27b,
27t, 36-37c, 37t, 38-39 all. Everett Collection: 32-33 all. Library of
Congress: 2, 4t, 4-5c, 5t, 6-7 all, 10-11c, 11t, 12-13b, 13t, 14-15 all,
16b, 17b, 18-19 all, 20-21 all, 22-23 all, 24-25 all, 28-29 all, 36t, 37cr.